DATE DUE

3 24571 0900496 4
Krumenauer, Heidi.

Rihanna

**921
RIH**

C_i

Blue Banner Biography

Rihanna

Heidi Krumenauer

Mitchell Lane
PUBLISHERS

P.O. Box 196
Hockessin, Delaware 19707
Visit us on the web: www.mitchelllane.com
Comments? email us: mitchelllane@mitchelllane.com

92/4
RIA C1 2011 18.50

Mitchell Lane PUBLISHERS

Printing 3 4 5 6 7 8 9

Blue Banner Biographies

Akon	Alan Jackson	Alicia Keys
Allen Iverson	Ashanti	Ashlee Simpson
Ashton Kutcher	Avril Lavigne	Bernie Mac
Beyoncé	Bow Wow	Brett Favre
Britney Spears	Carrie Underwood	Chris Brown
Chris Daughtry	Christina Aguilera	Christopher Paul Curtis
Ciara	Clay Aiken	Condoleezza Rice
Corbin Bleu	Daniel Radcliffe	David Ortiz
Derek Jeter	Eminem	Eve
Fergie (Stacy Ferguson)	50 Cent	Gwen Stefani
Ice Cube	Jamie Foxx	Ja Rule
Jay-Z	Jennifer Lopez	Jessica Simpson
J. K. Rowling	Johnny Depp	JoJo
Justin Berfield	Justin Timberlake	Kanye West
Kate Hudson	Keith Urban	Kelly Clarkson
Kenny Chesney	Lance Armstrong	Lindsay Lohan
Mariah Carey	Mario	Mary J. Blige
Mary-Kate and Ashley Olsen	Michael Jackson	Miguel Tejada
Missy Elliott	Nancy Pelosi	Nelly
Orlando Bloom	P. Diddy	Paris Hilton
Peyton Manning	Queen Latifah	**Rihanna**
Ron Howard	Rudy Giuliani	Sally Field
Sean Kingston	Selena	Shakira
Shirley Temple	Soulja Boy Tell 'Em	Taylor Swift
Timbaland	Tim McGraw	Toby Keith
Usher	Vanessa Anne Hudgens	Zac Efron

Library of Congress Cataloging-in-Publication Data
Krumenauer, Heidi.
  Rihanna / by Heidi Krumenauer.
    p. cm. — (Blue banner biography)
  Includes bibliographical references (p.) and index.
  ISBN 978-1-58415-673-4 (library bound)
  1. Rihanna, 1988– — Juvenile literature. 2. Singers—Juvenile literature. I. Title.
ML3930.R44K78 2009
782.42164092 — dc22
  [B]

2008008699

ABOUT THE AUTHOR: Heidi Krumenauer began writing newspaper articles as a teenager and continues to freelance in addition to working full-time in a management position with a Fortune 400 insurance company. She has written more than 1,000 articles and has contributed chapters to eight books. Her first book, *Why Does Grandma Have a Wibble?* was released in 2007. She is also the author of *Sean Kingston* and *Brett Favre* for Mitchell Lane Publishers. Heidi and her husband, Jeff, are raising their two sons in southern Wisconsin.

PUBLISHER'S NOTE: The following story has been thoroughly researched, and to the best of our knowledge represents a true story. While every possible effort has been made to ensure accuracy, the publisher will not assume liability for damages caused by inaccuracies in the data and makes no warranty on the accuracy of the information contained herein. This story has not been authorized or endorsed by Rihanna.

PLB / PLB2 / PLB2,29,30

Blue Banner Biography

Rihanna released her second album, A Girl Like Me, *in April 2006. By the end of 2007, the album had sold more than 3 million copies worldwide.*

Lucky Girl

*E*very now and then being in the right place at the right time can change your life. Nobody knows that better than Barbados beauty Rihanna. In December 2003, fifteen-year-old Rihanna was introduced to New York–based producer Evan Rogers. Evan was vacationing in Barbados with his wife, Jackie, when he was introduced to Rihanna by a mutual friend. Rogers is no stranger to talent. He and his production/songwriting partner, Carl Sturken, are a Grammy-nominated team who have produced hits for *American Idol*'s Ruben Studdard, 'NSync, Rod Stewart, Jessica Simpson, Kelly Clarkson, former Spice Girl Emma Bunton (Baby Spice), and Christina Aguilera.

During their brief meeting, Rihanna demonstrated her talent by singing "Emotion," a 2001 hit by Destiny's Child. Rogers knew immediately that her sweet voice and beauty were exactly what the music industry was looking for. He suggested that Rihanna travel to New York to record a few songs. At first, Rihanna's parents were unwilling to let her go, but after some thought they realized this would be a great opportunity for her. A few months later, Rihanna was on a plane to the United States for a recording session.

Over the next several months, Rihanna worked on her demo tape. She hoped it would be good enough to impress the record companies and maybe even land a contract. In January 2005, Rihanna left Barbados permanently and moved to New York City to pursue a new career. Rogers sent Rihanna's demo to all the major record labels. It was quickly given a lot of attention by Def Jam's CEO Shawn "Jay-Z" Carter. He arranged to meet Rihanna to discuss signing her with his record label, Def Jam Records. Rihanna was very nervous about singing for Jay-Z. "I was shaking, but he's such a cool person that he made it all very comfortable for me," she said.

> Rihanna was very nervous about singing for Jay-Z. "I was shaking, but he's such a cool person that he made it all very comfortable for me," she said.

During her audition, Rihanna sang "The Last Time," "Pon De Replay," and Whitney Houston's version of "For the Love of You." Jay-Z was very impressed with Rihanna's young talent and realized within minutes that she was going to be a huge success. "She had it all in her eyes," he said. "The way she carried herself and performed right there on the spot, I was like, 'Wow, she's a star. We'll figure out the rest later.' " Jay-Z was not going to let her go. He was eager to welcome Rihanna to one of the most popular record labels in the country.

Unlike most music artists who spend weeks—even months—negotiating business plans with record labels, Rihanna signed a contract with Def Jam Records within hours

Shawn "Jay-Z" Carter signed Rihanna to her first record deal with Def Jam Records in 2005. Jay-Z was the CEO of Def Jam Records at the time.

of her audition. "We wouldn't let her out of the building," Jay-Z said. "We actually closed all the doors and brought her some food. She brought in her lawyers and her production team, and we signed the deal that day."

On August 30, 2005, Rihanna's debut album, *Music of the Sun*, was released. "Pon De Replay," a track from the album, was a hit, reaching number 2 on the Billboard Hot 100. Less than eight months later, in April 2006, her second album, *A Girl Like Me*, was released.

Her big break with Def Jam was only the beginning to a whirlwind music career. At age sixteen, Rihanna was on her way to becoming a star!

> *Her big break with Def Jam was only the beginning to a whirlwind music career. At age sixteen, Rihanna was on her way to becoming a star!*

Island Girl

Rihanna (pronounced ree-AH-nuh) was born Robyn Rihanna Fenty on February 20, 1988. Although she doesn't think she was named after anyone in particular, she was told once that her name means "beautiful one." In Arabic, it means "Sweet Basil."

Rihanna was born in St. Michael, a parish of the small Caribbean island of Barbados. The island is hot and lush. As a citizen of Barbados, Rihanna is called a Barbadian (Bar-BAY-dee-an), or Bajan.

Like most natives of Barbados, Rihanna grew up speaking Standard English, especially when talking formally or with tourists. But when she spoke with her parents and her two younger brothers, Rorrey and Rajad, and the other island natives, they often used a different language called Bajan, which is sometimes called Barbadian Creole. The words are similar to those in the English language, but they are not as structured. Americans visiting Barbados would probably not understand what the natives are saying— although the Bajans have no trouble understanding one another.

Rihanna is proud of her language. The title of her worldwide smash hit "Pon De Replay" is taken from Bajan. *Pon* means "on," *de* means "the," and *replay* means the same in English. So "Pon De Replay" is telling the deejay to put the song *on the replay*, or "Play It Again"!

At seven years old, Rihanna discovered she had a good voice. She told her mother, "I wanna do this for real."

Rihanna's island childhood was considered quiet and average. Her father, Ronald, who is Irish-Barbadian, was a store supervisor. Her mother, Monica, who is Guyanese-Barbadian, was an accountant. Rihanna has talked openly about her father's drug addiction and the problems it caused her family. She's also talked about the stressful times in her home when her parents were married. When her parents finally divorced, Rihanna admits they felt relieved. "There was a lot of stress when we were together," she said. "I love them, but it was stressful and there was pressure. I started having head-aches . . . and after they separated for good, the headaches went away."

Growing up on the small island, Rihanna was considered a typical Bajan girl. She attended Charles F. Broome Memorial School (primary school) and later Combermere School (secondary school). She hung out on the beach with her friends and her brothers. She loved to sing, but her vocal training and professional performances were limited to her bedroom. She would hold a broom like a microphone stand and, pretending she was famous, entertain an imaginary audience in her room.

At seven years old, Rihanna discovered she had a good voice. She told her mother, "I wanna do this for real." At the time, her neighbors might have disagreed. "My neighbors would complain . . . they always knew when I was home," she said. In an interview on ABC's *The View*, Rihanna admitted that the neighbors could hear her singing in the shower. "I was pretty loud. I don't regret it, and I'm sure they don't regret it now either."

As a little girl, Rihanna knew that she would like to entertain crowds with her singing talent when she grew up. In her teens, Rihanna was fortunate to launch a music career that would make her an international icon.

Rihanna picks sea grapes in her hometown of St. Michael, Barbados.

Rihanna loved music and was soaking in all the local musical influences by learning a mix of calypso, reggae, and American hip-hop. Still, she was just an average girl with a dream—a dream to sing in front of a crowd. When she attended the prestigious Combermere School, she formed a musical trio with two of her classmates. In 2004, Rihanna chose to sing a song in the talent competition for the Miss Combermere Pageant—which she won. And in November 2004, she performed at the Colours of Combermere School show, singing Mariah Carey's "Hero."

Home is never too far for Rihanna, though. She makes sure that Barbados is in a little piece of everything she does.

"Early on, I developed a passion for [music]," Rihanna told *Teen Vogue*. "At first my mom was like, 'No way,' because in Barbados entertainers can only go so far. But I had a much bigger picture in my head. I was thinking international!"

Rihanna is enjoying her new life as a superstar, but, she says, "I miss so much. I miss home. I miss The Boatyard—that's my favorite club. I miss my friends. I miss my two younger brothers. I miss the beach and the food."

Home is never too far for Rihanna, though. She makes sure that Barbados is in a little piece of everything she does. The title of her 2005 album, *Music of the Sun*, has special meaning. "The word *sun* represents my culture where I'm from, the Caribbean. It represents me. So the album consists of music of the sun," she says.

Tomboy Turned Cover Girl

*F*rom head to toe, Rihanna has what it takes to be a star. A beautiful smile. Long legs. A trendy wardrobe. A popular haircut. And a stunning voice. She has been turning heads ever since she arrived in the United States in 2005. She has partnered with several major companies, topping the charts with more than just her music.

In 2007, Rihanna was named spokesperson for CoverGirl Cosmetics. She joins several other CoverGirl celebrities — including Queen Latifah, Tyra Banks, Faith Hill, and Brandy — as a model for the company. Gina Drosos, vice president and general manager of Global Cosmetics, Procter & Gamble Beauty (the company that owns CoverGirl), knew Rihanna would represent the beauty line well. "Rihanna is a talented, confident young woman who exemplifies the CoverGirl ideals with her inner confidence and fresh beauty. We're proud to welcome her to the CoverGirl family."

Rihanna wasn't always a beauty queen. Until her early teens, she was a tomboy, and makeup wasn't part of her daily routine. Even if Rihanna had wanted to, her mom wouldn't let her wear makeup because she was too young. Now, she's very excited to be a part of the CoverGirl celebrity lineup and admits that she never leaves home without her favorite makeup product—eye concealer.

To look at her perfectly toned body, her flawless skin, and her silky hair, one would think that Rihanna wakes up every morning looking like a magazine model. Not every day is a good one, though. Just like everyone, Rihanna has moments when she, too, feels like an ugly duckling. "Every woman has

With a busy schedule, Rihanna misses hanging out with her younger brothers, Rorrey and Rajad. On August 14, 2007, she was able to take a few minutes in the People Music Lounge for time with Rajad.

a fat day," Rihanna told *Giant* magazine. "Every woman has an ugly day. Every woman has a day when they ask, 'Where did these five pimples come from all of a sudden?' I hate those days."

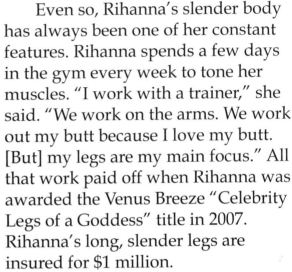

Even though her look was beautiful, Rihanna was bored with it. Wanting to distance herself from her peers, she cut her hair.

Even so, Rihanna's slender body has always been one of her constant features. Rihanna spends a few days in the gym every week to tone her muscles. "I work with a trainer," she said. "We work on the arms. We work out my butt because I love my butt. [But] my legs are my main focus." All that work paid off when Rihanna was awarded the Venus Breeze "Celebrity Legs of a Goddess" title in 2007. Rihanna's long, slender legs are insured for $1 million.

When Rihanna hit the music scene in 2005, the media liked to highlight her "island girl" appearance. With a curvy figure, sparkling eyes, and long wavy hair, Rihanna brought a new look that was turning heads. Even though her look was beautiful, Rihanna was bored with it. She wanted a change. Wanting to distance herself from her peers, she cut her hair. Her production team didn't like the idea, but Rihanna did it anyway. "I felt like a lot of it was because we all had a similar look; we were all classified as R&B girls. I just wanted to get a little edgy and cut my hair, and I didn't really ask anybody to do it. I just did it, changed myself completely, my image and everything. I just did it like a bad girl would do it."

Rihanna's risky move didn't hurt her image at all. Long hair or short, it seemed that everyone loved her beauty. They

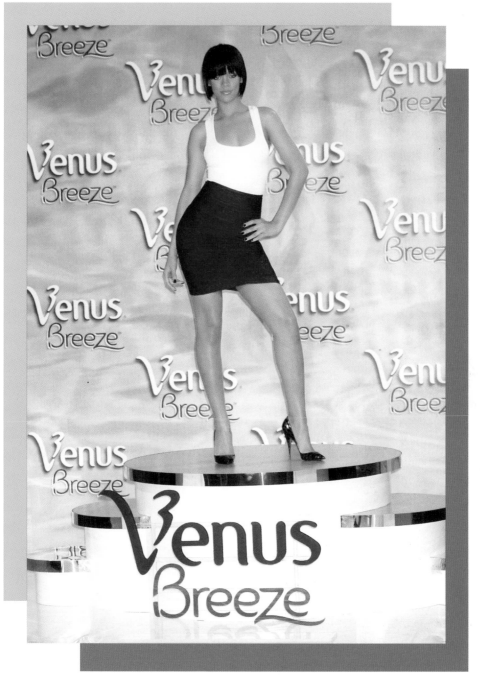

On June 8, 2007, Rihanna was presented with the Venus Breeze Celebrity Legs of a Goddess title. She keeps her million-dollar legs in shape by working out with a trainer.

Rihanna is known all over the world for her keen and trendy fashion sense. Early in her singing career, she wore baggy jeans — a style she no longer embraces.

loved her fashion sense, too. Magazines all over the world have scooped up Rihanna for their covers, including *Cosmopolitan*, *Allure*, *Teen Vogue*, *Fashion*, *Elle*, *Seventeen*, *You*, *Paper*, and *Fashion18*. She's also been spotted on the covers of *Giant*, *Jewel*, *Complex*, *Vibe*, *FHM*, and *Maxim*.

So how does Rihanna describe her style? She told *Seventeen* that it's never the same; she likes to switch it up and take risks. "I don't like to follow trends as much as I like to set trends," she said. Rihanna started thinking about style at an early age, reading fashion and teen magazines when she was growing up in Barbados. Today, Rihanna's signature style is that she doesn't like to wear the same kind of thing twice.

Even though she is becoming as well known for her fashion as her music, she admits that she's still "a little tomboyish." She has not always been comfortable having a sexy image and said that when she first started singing, she was wearing baggy jeans. As she looks back, Rihanna said, "How could I have worn those baggy jeans and think it was cool?"

> *Rihanna's risky move didn't hurt her image at all. Long hair or short, it seemed that everyone loved Rihanna's beauty.*

Baggy jeans or slinky dress, Rihanna knows how to get attention!

CHAPTER 4

A Girl Hitting the High Notes

*S*he has played to thousands of dedicated fans from New York City to Los Angeles. She has even belted out the high notes to crowds in Japan, Singapore, Canada, and Nigeria. In September 2007, she was nominated for five MTV Video Awards, bringing home two, for Monster Single and Video of the Year. In less than two years, Rihanna had reached what it takes most music hopefuls a lifetime to achieve. And this was just the beginning for this Bajan beauty who plans to stay at the top for a very long time!

Growing up, Rihanna was exposed to a lot of reggae music because her mother ran a reggae club. Her favorite reggae artists are Sizzla, Spice Cartel, Bob Marley, and Damian Marley, and they continue to influence her music.

Other than the club, Rihanna was influenced by a host of popular R&B singers. Day and night, she listened to Celine Dion, Mariah Carey, Whitney Houston, Brandy, Alicia Keys, and Beyoncé. They, too, have contributed to Rihanna's special blend of talent.

Rihanna has a great ear for success, and that rang true when she heard a track for "Umbrella." She just knew that

In 2007, Rihanna won two MTV Music Awards – Video of the Year and Monster Single of the Year for her song "Umbrella." She knew the song would be a hit.

song was for her, and she wasn't about to let any other singer take it to the top of the charts.

"It is funny because I heard the song the night before the Grammys. I knew I wanted the song," Rihanna said. "I was like, 'The song is mine. I have to have it.' I listened to it all day, getting ready for the Grammys. Then that night at the after-party, I saw the manager who manages the producers. I saw him and was like, 'This song is my song. "Umbrella" is mine.' He kind of laughed it off. I held his face like, 'No. Listen to me. "Umbrella" is my song.' I prayed about it and kept my fingers crossed. I had a lot of people fighting for it behind me and we eventually got it."

Jay-Z had the same intuition as Rihanna, saying: "I knew it was going to be a number one record. I believe what happened with this album is that she found her voice."

It's a good thing Rihanna was so persistent. With several other music artists on the list to record the single, Rihanna landed the deal. "Umbrella," featuring Jay-Z, is on Rihanna's third studio album, *Good Girl Gone Bad*. When "Umbrella" was released as a single on March 29, 2007, it debuted at the top of the Billboard Hot 100 chart in the U.S. and stayed there for seven consecutive weeks. "Umbrella" also topped the European charts. Because of the success and popularity of this song, Rihanna has launched a new line of umbrellas with Totes Company.

> *So how do you describe Rihanna's music? Is it hip-hop? Reggae? R&B? Rihanna would say "Yes!" to them all.*

So how do you describe Rihanna's music? Is it hip-hop? Reggae? R&B? Rihanna would say "Yes!" to them all. Actually, she makes a great comparison when she tries to describe the blend of her music. Her mother makes a Bajan dish consisting of all types of meats. Rihanna compares her music to this dish—her favorite meal—saying that her music is much like that. It consists of a lot of things, from reggae to hip-hop to R&B to soca. (Soca is dance music that combines soul and calypso music; it is popular in Barbados.)

Rihanna credits Gwen Stefani with changing her perspective on music. When on tour with Gwen, Rihanna learned that it was all right to try a little of everything. "It was hard for me to choose what I wanted to do. She likes all

Rihanna performed "Umbrella" at the 2007 World Music Awards held in Monaco. She also took home three awards: Entertainer of the Year, Best-Selling R&B Female Artist, and Best-Selling Pop Female Artist. Awards were presented based on record sales instead of popular votes.

types of music and so do I, so on my album there's a lot of that going on."

Rihanna likes to keep her music fresh and admits the new sound on *Good Girl Gone Bad* is not as playful; it's more rock star. "I thought it would be fun to get out of the innocent, generic shell that everyone molds me into."

Rihanna's blend of musical styles is obviously working for her. On December 12, 2007, she and her platinum album, *Good Girl Gone Bad*, captured her six Grammy nominations.

Good Girl Gone Bad?

*T*here's nothing bad about this good girl. In fact, while many superstars have chosen drugs, drinking, or other destructive habits as a way to rebel, Rihanna has chosen a different path—one that doesn't land her in the tabloid magazines. "I'm setting a great example for girls," she said. "I just want to lead them in the right direction." And Rihanna has chosen to help others. In 2006, she created the nonprofit organization Believe, which provides medical services, school supplies, and toys for children in need.

Rihanna is a little rebellious, but not in a bad way. When she decided to cut her hair and change her image in 2007, she said the title of her third album, *Good Girl Gone Bad* (released June 5, 2007), is a reflection of where she is in her life and the changes she's making. "I just got a little rebellious—I think it's about time. I got tired of that generic image that I used to have and I just want to be more edgy." Rihanna adds that she wants to be funky and have more fun. "I don't care who likes it, who hates it. I like it. I just want to do what I want. I just had to break away from that innocent girly image that I used to have."

Rihanna hangs with some of her fans at a Charity Meet and Greet for her Believe Foundation. Rihanna founded Believe in 2006 to ensure the health and well-being of children.

Girly-girl is not how most people would describe a video shoot she did for her hit single "Umbrella." One video scene required Rihanna to be painted in silver. With her body almost completely covered in paint, she said, "I felt free. It was a pretty cool thing to do. I never thought in a million years that I would paint myself up to my nostrils in silver and do a video. It was fantastic."

Always looking for new outlets of self-expression, Rihanna has become fond of tattoos. Being in the spotlight, posing for magazine covers, and portraying an image with CoverGirl, Rihanna listens to the warnings of her management team. They have provided advice about where the tattoos should be located on her body and where they shouldn't. They remind her often that she has a "look" to uphold.

While Rihanna receives a lot of advice, everyone knows that she will do what she wants to do. She listens to her team, but she is the one in control of her life, and she's proud of it! When asked about the process for recording her new album, Rihanna was quick to respond: "I have all the freedom I could ever ask for. Not that they gave it to me. I was just taking it. That's why it's called *Good Girl Gone Bad*. I wasn't about listening to what anyone wanted me to look like, or sound like or act like."

> While Rihanna receives a lot of advice, everyone knows that she will do what she wants to do.

Outside the spotlight, Rihanna isn't considered good or bad — she's just an average down-to-earth girl. In her spare time, she loves to watch TV (especially *Grey's Anatomy*), listen to music, and catch up on sleep. She loves to shop. She doesn't even have a bodyguard whizzing her in and out of top-of-the-line shopping boutiques. She can do that on her own.

When she's not singing or hanging out, Rihanna is thinking about her next venture. "Clothing, swimsuits, lingerie," she said. "I want to design. I have to be involved because I'm very creative." After a role in the movie *Bring It On: All or Nothing* in 2006 and appearances on the TV shows *Las Vegas* and *All My Children*, Rihanna hasn't ruled out acting. She doesn't want anything too boring, though. She'd prefer horror, action, or drama roles. It looks like Rihanna is the real deal, and if she has her way, she will be around a long while.

In February 2008, Rihanna and Jay-Z received a Grammy Award for the Best Rap/Sung Collaboration for the hit song "Umbrella."

Even with a glamorous lifestyle and hit records, this "real deal" who is topping the music charts says she still feels funny giving autographs to her fans. Rihanna recalls one of the first times she gave autographs to a crowd of people on the street. "It felt so good and weird. They were even apologizing. They said, 'Sorry to bother you, but can I please have your autograph?' I'm like, 'Don't apologize, I want to give you my autograph.' "

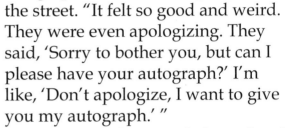

"Keep good people around you, because if you have a strong circle, then it's hard for negativity to get in," Jay-Z told her.

Rihanna's fans are dedicated and are often overcome with joy when they meet her. Rihanna realized she was a superstar when she encountered fans who started crying when they met her. "That freaks me out because I don't know what to do. One girl in Barbados started screaming when we met, and the more I hugged her, the more she was screaming. I was like 'Uh-oh.' "

Rihanna's superstardom has her running from coast to coast and from continent to continent. At times, playing her popular role in the entertainment industry gets a little crazy and stressful, but Rihanna is enjoying the ride. As music stars come and go, Rihanna is aware that her red-hot career can fizzle at any moment—and that keeps her grounded. "I just try to think about the fun in it. You have to have fun or you'll go crazy."

She also keeps in mind the best advice she ever received from her mentor, Jay-Z. "Keep good people around you, because if you have a strong circle, then it's hard for negativity to get in."

CHRONOLOGY

1988   Robyn Rihanna Fenty is born to Ronald and Monica Fenty on February 20 in St. Michael, Barbados.

1995   She tells her mother she wants to be a professional singer.

2003   Rihanna is introduced to record producer Evan Rogers while he is vacationing in Barbados. He asks her to record a demo in the United States.

2004   Rihanna wins the Miss Combermere Pageant; she records a demo in the United States.

2005   Rihanna moves to the U.S. and auditions for Def Jam CEO, Shawn "Jay-Z" Carter. Within hours, she is offered a record contract. Her first album, *Music of the Sun*, is released in August.

2006   Eight months after her first album, Rihanna's second album, *A Girl Like Me*, is released. Rihanna lands a couple of small roles on NBC's drama *Las Vegas* and ABC's daytime soap opera *All My Children*. She also has a role in the movie *Bring It On: All or Nothing*. She founds the charity Believe.

2007   In June, her third album, *Good Girl Gone Bad*, is released, and Rihanna launches her first ads for CoverGirl Cosmetics. She is awarded the Venus Breeze "Celebrity Legs of a Goddess" title. Her legs are insured for $1 million by Lloyd's of London. In September, she receives five MTV Music Award nominations; she brings home the awards for Monster Single and Video of the Year for "Umbrella." By December, *Good Girl Gone Bad* has sold more than three million copies worldwide. Rihanna and *Good Girl Gone Bad* receive six Grammy nominations.

2008   Rihanna wins her first Grammy Award. She is nominated for the NAACP Image Award. *Good Girl Gone Bad* wins Canada's Juno Award for International Album of the Year.

2009   After escaping an abusive relationship with Chris Brown, Rihanna releases her fourth album, *Rated R*.

ACHIEVEMENTS

Discography

Albums
2009 *Rated R*
2007 *Good Girl Gone Bad*
2006 *A Girl Like Me*
2005 *Music of the Sun*

Singles
2009 "Russian Roulette"
2008 "Disturbia"
       "Take a Bow"
2007 "Umbrella"
       "Shut Up and Drive"
       "Don't Stop the Music"
       "Hate That I Love You"
       "Breakin' Dishes"

Filmography
2006 *Bring It On: All or Nothing*

2006 "SOS"
       "Unfaithful"
       "We Ride"
       "Break It Off"
       "Roll It" (J-Status featuring
          Rihanna)
2005 "Pon De Replay"
       "If It's Lovin' That You Want"

Awards
2008 American Music Award: Favorite Pop/Rock Female Artist
       American Music Award: Favorite Soul/R&B Female Artist
       Grammy Award: Best Rap/Sung Collaboration—"Umbrella"

2007 World Music Awards: Best-Selling R&B Female Artist
       World Music Awards: Best-Selling Pop Female Artist
       World Music Awards: Female Entertainer of the Year
       American Music Awards: Favorite Female Artist-Soul/R&B
       Teen Choice Awards: Choice Music: R&B Artist
       MTV Music Awards: "Monster Single"
       MTV Music Awards: "Video of the Year"
       MOBO Awards: Best International Act

2006 Teen Choice Awards: Female Breakout Artist
       Teen Choice Awards: Choice R&B Artist
       MOBO Awards: Best R&B Artist
       Billboard Music Awards: Female Artist of the Year
       Billboard Music Awards: Pop 100 Artist of the Year
       Billboard Music Awards: Hot 100 Artist of the Year

FURTHER READING

If you enjoyed this book about Rihanna, you might also enjoy these Blue Banner Biographies about some of the other people mentioned in the story:

Bankston, John. *Alicia Keys*. Hockessin, Delaware: Mitchell Lane Publishers, 2005.
Bankston, John. *Jay-Z*. Hockessin, Delaware: Mitchell Lane Publishers, 2005.
Tracy, Kathleen. *Gwen Stefani*. Hockessin, Delaware: Mitchell Lane Publishers, 2007.
Tracy, Kathleen. *Mariah Carey*. Hockessin, Delaware: Mitchell Lane Publishers, 2007.
Tracy, Kathleen. *Queen Latifah*. Hockessin, Delaware: Mitchell Lane Publishers, 2005.

Works Consulted
"A Huge Year for Rihanna." DefJam.com, December 12, 2007,
    http://www.defjam.com/site/news.php?news_id=104510
AP Entertainment: Rihanna sound bite, June 8, 2007.
    http://www.aparchive.com/aparchive/index.html
Coppa, Matt. "Q&A: Rihanna." *Star*, October 8, 2007, p. 82.
Crossingham, John. "Red Hot Rihanna." *Fashion*, October, 2007.
Deem, Megan. "Tough Love." *Elle*, July 2007, p. 175.
Drew, Ian. "This Minute You Want To Know About . . ." *US*, September 3, 2007,
    p. 76.
Ellen DeGeneres Show, December 14, 2007.
Hoard, Christian. "Rihanna Brings Riddims." *Rolling Stone*, August 18, 2005.
"Interview with Rihanna." Kidzworld.com http://www.kidzworld.com/
    article/5853-rihanna-interview
Jones, Bomani. "Rihanna Signs with CoverGirl." *Vibe*, December 5, 2006.
Orloff, Brian. "Rihanna Reveals How She Got Buff." *People*, June 2007.
People: "Behind the Scenes . . . at a Shoot with Rihanna." June 11, 2007, p. 160.
PRNewswire: "Venus Breeze Bestows Best Legs Honor Upon Rihanna." June 8, 2007.
Reuters: "Chart-topper Rihanna Rebels with Haircut." June 9, 2007.
Rosenberg, Carissa. "Rihanna Style Star." *Seventeen*, December/January 2008,
    pp. 65–67.
Serena, Kim. "Rihanna: Punked!" *Giant*, 2007, http://www.giantmag.com/content.
    php?cid=142
Smith, Beverly. "The Good, The Bad, The Rihanna." *Paper*, July 2007,
    http://www.papermag.com/?section=article&parid=2055
Star: "Rihanna Rocks." June 1, 2007, p.13.
Swash, Rosie. "Interview: Rihanna." *The Observer*, December 9, 2007,
    http://observer.guardian.co.uk/
The View, June 11, 2007.
Waterman, Lauren. "She's Got the Beat." *Teen Vogue*, November 2007, p. 168.

On the Internet
Rihanna's Official Site—http://www.rihannanow.com
Rihanna's MySpace Page—http://www.myspace.com/rihanna

INDEX